Greatest Misteaks

Move to the head of the class with word puzzles to help you pass!

by Kristi Thom

★ American Girl®

Published by American Girl Publishing
Copyright © 2012 by American Girl

Questions or comments? Call 1-800-845-0005, visit **americangirl.com**, or write to Customer Service,
American Girl, 8400 Fairway Place, Middleton, WI 53562-0497.

Printed in China
12 13 14 15 16 17 18 19 LEO 10 9 8 7 6 5 4 3 2 1

Editorial Development: Trula Magruder
Art Direction and Design: Camela Decaire
Production: Jeannette Bailey, Tami Kepler, Judith Lary, Kendra Schluter
Illustrations: Thu Thai at Arcana Studios

Dear Reader,

Welcome to Innerstar University! At this imaginary, one-of-a-kind school, you can live with your friends in a dorm called Brightstar House and find lots of fun ways to let your true talents shine.

This book is full of letters, posters, notes, signs, and other items from all around the Innerstar U campus. What makes them unusual is that they are all full of mistakes. Read the directions for each one and see if you can solve the puzzles and find all of the errors. In the process, you might learn a little bit about grammar and writing, and you'll get to know what Innerstar U and its students are like.

If you get stuck or just want to check your answers, turn to answers, starting on page 72. Have a good time looking for misteaks! Then head to www.innerstarU.com for even more games and fun.

Your friends at American Girl

PS: Did you catch the mistake in this letter? In the next-to-last line, "misteaks" should be "mistakes"!

Innerstar Guides

Every girl needs a few good friends to help her find her way.
These are the friends who are always there for you.

Emmy

A brave girl who loves
swimming and boating

Isabel

A confident girl with a
funky sense of style

Riley

A good sport, on the
field and off

Paige

A nature lover who leads hikes
and campus cleanups

Amber

An animal lover and a loyal friend

Neely

A creative girl who loves dance, music, and art

Logan

A super-smart girl who is curious about EVERYTHING

Shelby

A kind girl who is there for her friends—and loves making NEW friends!

Innerstar U Campus

1. Rising Star Stables
2. Star Student Center
3. Brightstar House
4. Starlight Library
5. Sparkle Studios
6. Blue Sky Nature Center

7. Real Spirit Center
8. Five-Points Plaza
9. Starfire Lake & Boathouse
10. U-Shine Hall
11. Good Sports Center
12. Shopping Square
13. The Market
14. Morningstar Meadow

Table of Contents

Check it out, and then check it off!

Brightstar House

Good Sports Center

Rising Star Stables

Sparkle Studios

U-Shine Hall

Answers start on page 72.

Meet Logan

Work side by side with your Innerstar University guide.

At Innerstar University, Logan loves school, likes to read, and studies many subjects.

Because of Logan's eagle eye, intelligence, and passion to help others, she's a great tutor at the library's help desk—she may even have helped you out once or twice if you visited the Innerstar University campus.

Now Logan wants to inspire you with her love for words— from editing and English to writing and recall. She'll walk you around campus, offer tips, and show you the many places mistakes can crop up in everyday life. You might even discover that you have a knack for editing, writing, and teaching others, too!

Brightstar House

Mixed-Up Message

Emmy left a message for Logan about their plans for the afternoon. She wrote it full of *homonyms*, which are words that sound alike but have different meanings and spellings. See if you can figure out what the note says and write it correctly.

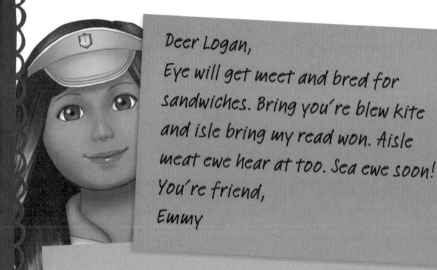

Deer Logan,
Eye will get meet and bred for sandwiches. Bring you're blew kite and isle bring my read won. Aisle meat ewe hear at too. Sea ewe soon!
You're friend,
Emmy

DearD iary

Neely listened to music while typing in her online diary, so she got distracted and put spaces in the wrong places. Figure out where they should go, and then correct the document by using proofreading symbols. Use a line | to mark a word break and ⌒ to close up a space. We've done a couple for you.

Dear D iary,

Toda ywa sagrea tda y.Iwen ttoS park leStu dios t om eetso mefrien dsan dmak ecraf ts.Som eone inv ite dane w gir lnam edKa ylat ojoi nus.She jus tstart edher ean di skin dofsh y. Westa rted talk ingan dbefo reyo ukno wit,s hewa slaughi ngan d jok ingaro undwit hme. Iinvit edhe rt ogos wimm ing wit hm etomor row.Sh esee msreal lynic e,an dI' m gla dt ohav e an ewfri end.

Talkt oyo ula ter!

Neely

Neely's Nutty Note

Neely planned a unique thank-you letter for her grandma by writing her message on sticky notes and placing the notes on craft paper. To help finish the project, write the notes in their correct order at right.

I love that you made it yourself,

Thank you very much

Dear Grandma,

I hope you can teach me

and you used all my favorite colors.

Thanks again!

Love, Neely

to knit someday.

Until then, when I wear the sweater

for the cool sweater!

I'll think of you.

Good Sports Center

Really Silly Rules

Here's a crazy sign—the verbs (action words) are all in the wrong sentences. See if you can figure out where each underlined word belongs. Write the correct word in the space at the end of each sentence.

Good Sports Center Rules

1. Do not <u>lock</u> in the locker room. _____

2. Store your belongings in a locker and <u>shower</u> it. _____

3. Be sure to <u>tell</u> before entering pool. _____

4. <u>Run</u> wet towels in laundry bins. _____

5. <u>Put</u> only proper athletic shoes on the court. _____

6. After playing, <u>wear</u> sports equipment. _____

7. <u>Clean</u> a coach if you injure yourself. _____

Boo, Team!

The pom-pom team wrote new cheers, but someone messed with the words. Replace the underlined word or phrase in each line with its opposite to make the team's routine more cheerful.

Cheer 1

Feeling <u>ashamed</u>? _____

Yell it <u>quiet</u>— _____

<u>Stop</u>, team! _____

Cheer 2

<u>Sit down</u>, _____

Let me hear you <u>whisper</u>! _____

That's what <u>working by yourself</u> _____

Is <u>none</u> about! _____

Cheer 3

<u>Go to sleep</u>, everybody! _____

We're <u>there</u> to say _____

<u>Their</u> team's gonna win _____

And today is the <u>night</u>! _____

A word opposite in meaning to another word is its antonym. A way to remember that is "anti" means "against." Bad is against good, so "bad" and "good" are antonyms!

Numbers & Letters

Riley used texting shorthand on a note she left for Logan in the locker room. See if you can figure out what it says. Then rewrite the note with the correct words in the spaces below.

Logan,
Good news—R team 1! I waited 4 U
after the game, but I didn't C U. We
R going 4 pizza now, so Y don't U join
us? (Unless U already 8!)
Hope 2 C U soon.
Riley

Logan,
Good news—____ team ____! I waited ____
____ after the game, but I didn't ____ ____.
We ____ going ____ pizza now, so ____ don't
____ join us? (Unless ____ already ____!)
Hope __ ____ ____ soon.
Riley

Sports Seen

Logan went to a basketball game and saw lots of crazy mistakes, including the ones on the scoreboard! Can you find nine others in the scene below?

Rising Star Stables

Tack Track

Someone has moved the photos on how to tack up, or saddle, a horse, and now they're out of order. Number the photos in the order they should be.

Horse Sense

Amber must work the horses at different times today, but after reading her notes, she saw that someone incorrectly filled out the exercise chart. Read the notes below and correct the mistakes.

Silver Sky must be ridden after noon and Fleet before noon.

Angel needs to be ridden first and Rio needs to be walked last.

Silver Sky should be exercised immediately after Fleet.

COMET   ANGEL   RIO

	9 A.M.	11 A.M.	1 P.M.	3 P.M.	5 P.M.
SILVER SKY	no				
COMET	no				
ANGEL	yes	no	no	no	no
RIO	no				
FLEET	no				

	9 A.M.	11 A.M.	1 P.M.	3 P.M.	5 P.M.
SILVER SKY	yes	no	no	no	no
COMET	no	yes	no	no	yes
ANGEL	no	no	no	no	yes
RIO	no	no	yes	no	no
FLEET	no	no	no	yes	no

FLEET

SILVER SKY

Tricky Trophies

If you look inside the riding club's trophy case, you'll find 12 trophies and ribbons with mistakes. Circle them.

Innerstar University Ridding Club
Horse Show

1rd
PLACE

2nd
PIACE

3rd
PLASE

BEST IN SNOW

Apostrophe Catastrophe

Amber made a sign letting riders know about an upcoming horse show. Problem is, the apostrophe key on her computer was on the fritz. Add all the 13 missing apostrophes.

Its time for the
Horse Lovers Fun Show!

Mark your calendar
because you wont want to miss out.
Itll be July 2 at 3:00.
Well have events, games, prizes,
and even a parade.

Dont have a horse? Dont worry—well lend you
one from the riding clubs herd.

You cant beat that, so
theres no excuse for not
signing up. Youre going
to have a blast, and your
horse will be up
to its ears in fun.

**For more info,
talk to Amber—
shell help you out.**

Sparkle Studios

Art-Show Showdown

Neely is showing her paintings but still needs to add her titles. Read each title and write its number below the painting that it best fits. You have only 2 minutes before the doors open!

A. ◯

B. ◯

C. ◯

D. ◯

Titles

1. *Purple Shoes, Purple Bird, Green Flowers*
2. *Green Bird, Orange Heart, Blue Shoes*
3. *Purple Heart, Pink Flowers, Green Shoes*
4. *Blue Bird, Orange Flowers, Yellow Shoes*
5. *Green Heart, Pink Bird, Blue Flowers*
6. *Yellow Heart, Orange Shoes, Green Flowers*
7. *Pink Shoes, Green Bird, Blue Heart*
8. *Pink Heart, Purple Flowers, Orange Bird*

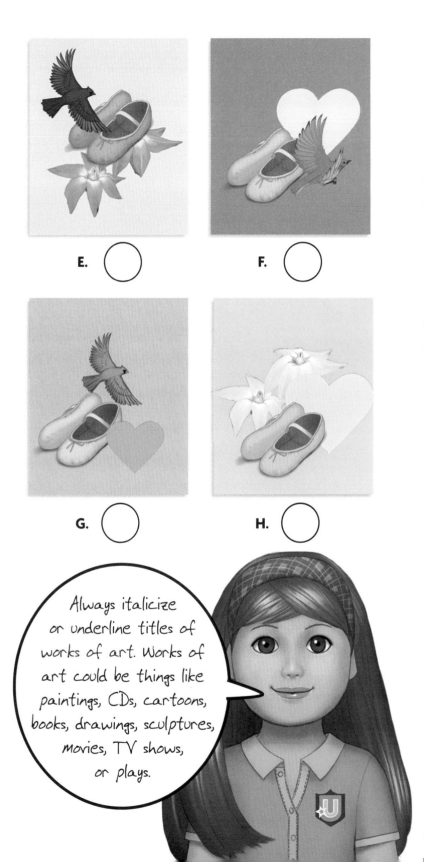

E. ◯   F. ◯

G. ◯   H. ◯

Always italicize or underline titles of works of art. Works of art could be things like paintings, CDs, cartoons, books, drawings, sculptures, movies, TV shows, or plays.

Rave Review

Shelby wrote a review of an art show. It doesn't have any mistakes in it, but it's a little dull. Read the review and replace the highlighted words with stronger descriptive words. Rewrite the review with the new words on the lines below.

A review of the show "Daydreams" by Shelby

I thought this show was nice. The artist used lots of colors in her artwork. One painting had sections of red, blue, and green. Another painting was big. One painting called *Floral Fantasy* had a bunch of flowers all over it. I liked seeing these paintings because they made me feel good.

A review of the show "Daydreams" by _____

_____

_____

_____

_____

_____

_____

Craft Crunch

Isabel went to Sparkle Studios to make an animal gift container for Amber, but the instructions got all jumbled. See if you can put them in the correct order.

Step ( ) Roll the tube in paw-print tissue paper, and secure along the tube with tape.

Step ( ) Start with an empty toilet paper tube.

Step ( ) Fill the wrapped tube with animal magnets, stickers, and a key chain.

Step ( ) To be certain the contents stay in the tube, tie the tissue ends with ribbon.

Supplies Surprise

The art supplies are all mixed up! One letter in each supply-bin label has been *added, taken away,* or *changed.* Write the correct supply name in the space provided.

1. grubber stamps

2. litter

3. taper

4. pinkpads

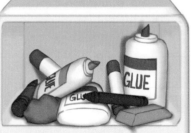

5. blue

6. aint

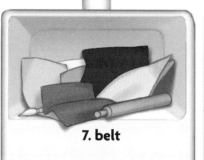

7. belt

8. gatercolors

9. rayons

10. makers

11. crushes

12. rules

13. sticklers

14. play

U-Shine Hall

Ticket Trouble

These tickets to the dance recital are pretty weird.
Circle all the mistakes you can find!

Dance Recital

Dance Recital

Admit nOne
"Dance Spectaculer"
Truesday, April 1rd
3:30 A.M.

Dance Recital

U Shine Hill
Row A
Seat 9 1/2
$10.00c

Saturday
3:00 p.m.

Program Problems

Innerstar University's
Dance Spectacular

Welcome Dance
All Dancers
An exciting number to thank you for coming to the show and to wish you a safe trip home

Tapping Trio
Isabel, Cleo, Haley, and Annika
These three will amaze you with their jazzy routine set to a slow classic played on piano.

Jewelry-Box Ballerina
Neely
Start the music box and watch this ballerina pirouette in her tap shoes!

Logan went to see the dance show and saw some big bloopers in the program. Circle all of the mistakes you find.

Jazz Junction
Shelby and Chloe
A very contemporary dance that your great-great-grandma used to do

Ballet Blossoms
Neely, Riley, Ella, and Linden
See these dancers turn into lovely blossoms from a vegetable tree.

Farewell Finale
All Dancers
An opening act that showcases all of the dancers in today's show!

Inspiration Station

Cool posters cover the dance studio walls, but their quotes need correcting. Circle the mispelled words. Note: One word on a poster is used wrong on purpose!

Dansing makes you're spirit fly.

Happy bithay tutu you!

Dance makes the word go rond.

Everyone has a little dancer in her hart.

A Chance to Dance

Neely wrote a note to let girls know about tryouts for the next dance show, but she was in a big hurry and forgot to put spaces in between words. Draw a line / where each space should be.

Attention,dancers!Ournext

danceshowwillbecalled

"DancingDreams."Itwillfeature

ballet,jazz,tap,andmoderndance.

TryoutswillbeFridayat

threeo'clockintheauditorium.Please

besuretobringyour

music.Tosignup,talktoNeely.

A slash line / is a proofreading mark that means "add a space here." Look for a list of other proofreading marks in the back of this book.

Pet Palooza

Name Game

All of the pets' names were on their pet beds, but the letters fell off and someone put them back incorrectly. Can you unscramble each animal's name?
Hint: All the pets are named after foods.

1. NO CUT CO

2. RAG US

3. REP PEP

4. SAY TOT

5. REN GIG

6. LINE RAP

7. I COOL TECH CHAP

8. HEY NO

Messy Message

A customer called **Pet Palooza** to get some information. Someone took the message in a hurry and didn't use any capital letters or punctuation. Can you make sense of the message? Circle the letters that should be capitalized, and add punctuation where it needs to go.

mrs chauncy called at one oclock she wants to know whether pet palooza can take care of her dog sweetie while she goes on vacation she is leaving in a week i told her i did not know if there would be room but i would check would someone please call her back her number is 5551876 she wants to know by tomorrow thanks so much

Not-Right Invite

Today Logan got an invitation to a birthday party in her mailbox. She found 16 mistakes in it! Circle them all.

Its a Doggone Surpize Birtday Party fer Amber!

Date: Wensday, April 31

Time: 3:00 o'clock

Were: Pet Palooza

RVSP to Paige bye Saterday

Dont tell Amber!

Insted of a prezent, pleese bring a dog or cat toy too donate.

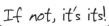

A common writing mistake occurs when using it's/its. Try this: If you can replace the word it's with it is or it has, most likely the word should be it's. If not, it's its!

Instruction Obstruction

Amber left instructions for how to care for the dogs and cats, but she wrote the instructions in a very confusing way. Rewrite each sentence using *only five (or fewer)* words. We've given an example on the first one.

Canines

1. Canines need to stroll outdoors with a person two times in 24 hours.

   .... *Walk dogs twice a day.* ....

2. Aquatic refreshment must continually be made available in the serving vessels provided.

   ....

3. In order to maintain canines' appearances, every time 48 hours pass, apply the bristled tool in a sweeping motion across their pelts.

   ....

4. All canines should be provided with playthings.

   ....

Felines

1. Do not allow 24 hours to pass without providing small tidbits to felines.

2. It is forbidden to allow felines to pass through the door into the world beyond.

3. Participate in amusing pastimes with felines.

4. Every seven days it is necessary to launder the objects on which the felines sleep.

Starlight Library

Title Trouble

Someone mixed up this list of book titles. Can you number them in alphabetical order?

_____Dance Across the Sky

_____Super Soccer Girl

_____Annabelle in Paris

_____Friendship Tales—Crazy but True!

_____Heaps of Handy Homework-Helping Hints

_____Ready, Set, Go Camping!

_____Horsey Heaven

_____Xylophone Repair for Fun and Profit

_____How to Make Spectacular Costumes

_____Kittens Lost in the Big City

Alphabetizing can be fun! Write identical words, phrases, or titles on two sets of index cards. Then compete with a friend to see who can order them the fastest!

Maga-zany Mix

Something crazy has happened to these magazines.
Circle the 13 mistakes found on the covers.

TWEEN GIRLS

51 WONDERFUL CHRISTMAS IDEAS!

SWEAT TREATS TO EAT

LEARN TO BE A BETTER DRIVER

August

PUPS & KITTIES MAGAZINE

Crafts Your Pet Will Love to Do

Teach an Old Hog New Tricks

FURRIE FRIENDS

Eagle Eyes

Logan was studying in the library when she noticed a spelling error and something else. Can you figure out both?

Cat Crazy

Kooky Comics

Summers in School

Girls Like Dogs

Into the Wild

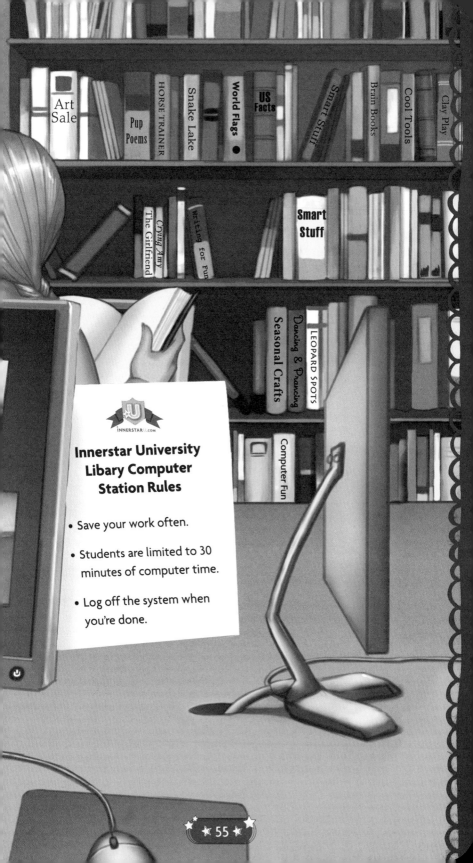

Art
Sale

Pup
Poems

HORSE TRAINER

Snake Lake

World Flags

US
Facts

Smart Stuff

Brain Books

Cool Tools

Clay Play

The Girlfriend

Crying Amy

Writing for Fun

Smart
Stuff

Seasonal Crafts

Dancing & Prancing

LEOPARD SPOTS

Computer Fun

**Innerstar University
Libary Computer
Station Rules**

- Save your work often.

- Students are limited to 30
  minutes of computer time.

- Log off the system when
  you're done.

INNERSTARU.COM

Spill Check

Logan was working at the help desk when a student brought her this book report. The girl said that her computer didn't find any problems with the spelling, but she thought there might be mistakes. Boy, was she right! Logan found 22. Circle them.

Gracie in the Bug City

This brook yells the story of Gracie, a girl whom moves from here family's farm to life with her ant in the big city for the simmer. At firs, Gracie has trouble baking friends. She also messes the firm and the animals. He doesn't like how crawdad and noisy the city is. Then she meats a girl named Janna in her compartment building. Janna shows Gracie tall the things she loaves about her city, like the sparks and the museums. Gracie is said when it's time to grow back home, but she's happy when Janna says shell come visit.

Sweet Treats Bakery

Muddled Menu

As a joke, someone messed with the menu at the Sweet Treats Bakery and replaced one word on each treat name with a rhyming word. Can you figure out the real names of the cupcakes?

Cupcake Crazy!

Try a treat any time of the day.
Fun frostings and fabulous flavors turn
dessert decisions into a piece of cake!

Cotton Sandy $1.75

Loco Cloud $1.75

Linty Dream $2.00

Gorilla Surprise $2.00

Head Velvet $3.00

Blueberry Gobbler.......$3.00

Lemon Flop $2.50

Hint Chocolate............$2.50

Strawberry Dream.......$3.00

Ferret Top $3.00

Ape Goodness..............$2.00

Sweet Bunny $2.00

Cripple Berry $3.00

Bumpkin Pie $2.50

Mutt Crunch $2.00

Loony Shopping List

While working at the Sweet Treats Bakery, Logan accidentally added her own shopping list to the store's. Cross off anything that you would never use to make cupcakes.

Shopping List

flour	hot dogs
flowers	straws
sugar	strawberries
tape	blueberries
vanilla	dinner rolls
butter	raspberries
bandages	bananas
envelopes	artichokes
ketchup	lemon juice
milk	tomato juice
eggs	peanut butter
pizza	peas
cocoa	mustard
tortillas	honey
chocolate chips	cream cheese
onions	mushrooms

1. walk your dog today!

2. give your pet a treat

3. A dog is a girl's best friend! ☺

Recipe Mess-Up

These baking instructions have some real problems. Some of the nouns have ended up in the wrong places! Take a close look and see if you can figure out where each underlined word belongs. Write the correct word in the space at the end of each sentence.

Cupcake Instructions

1. Read the <u>bowl</u> all the way through before you begin. _____

2. Gather all of the <u>batter</u> you'll need. _____

3. Wash your <u>frosting</u>. _____

4. Measure the ingredients into a <u>recipe</u>. _____

5. Use a <u>cupcake liners</u> to mix everything. _____

6. Place <u>hands</u> into the baking pan. _____

7. Pour the <u>timer</u> into the liners. _____

8. Set the <u>ingredients</u>. _____

9. After baking, let the cupcakes cool, and then decorate them with <u>spoon</u>. _____

Wrong Receipt

When Logan bought drinks and a snack, she got a receipt. She found lots of mistakes on it. Circle all of the errors you find.

Wellcome 2 Sweet Treets

Its the sweeetest place
at Innerstar Univesity

• •

Febuary 14

Strawbury copcake	$3.00 dollars
Extra sprinckles	$0.50
Pink lemonaid	$1.50 dollar
Iced tee	$1.50 dollar
Totally	$6.50
Amont tendered	$7.00
Change do	$0.75

Thank yoo four coming have an ice day!

• •

The smallest incorrect detail can ruin a day, such as misspelling a friend's name on her birthday card. Pay attention to the details.

Shopping
Square

Screwy Signs

Neely takes photos of signs she finds with mistakes.
Look at her collection and circle all of the mistakes you can find.

Good Sparts
Center

Shooping
Square

Tees Teasers

These T-shirts are on sale because they all have mistakes printed on them. Correct all the errors you can find.

Many editors have a list of commonly misspelled words at their desks. You can find a list in the back of this book. If you like, add your own misspellings to the list!

Its a great day!

a dog is a girls best friend

Your my B**EST** friend

To **CUTE** for my own good

BETTER SAFE THEN SORRY

Kitten's RULE

REDUCE REFUSE RECYLE

Lator Gator!

ONE SMART COOKY

Happy Birfhday

Proud to bee a BOOKWORM

i love Cheerleeding

Hairstyle How-To

A stylist at the hair salon keeps notecards with the
correct way to do a basic braid, but the cards got mixed up.
Can you put them back in the right order?
Write the correct number in front of each step.

Basic Braid

Then cross the section on your left over the center
section. Hold sections tightly as you cross them.

Tie off 1 pigtail. Separate hair from the other pigtail
into 3 equal sections.

Make a part down the back of your head for pigtails.

Continue crossing over the center section with right
and left sections until hair is braided. Tie off with an
elastic and repeat on the other side.

Cross the section on your right over the center
section.

Real Spirit Center

Body Basics

This sign was supposed to explain how yoga is good for the different parts of the body, but somehow eight body parts were replaced with rhyming words. Figure out which words should be body parts, and write them on the list.

YOGA

Good for the body and spirit!

Yoga strengthens your whole body, from your farms all the way down to your rose. Yoga can help you have better balance, so you can comfortably stand on one egg. Yoga can also improve your flexibility in your boulders, pack, fleas, and dips. Plus yoga can boost your concentration, which is good for your drain. Why not try yoga today?

....

....

....

....

Class Conundrum

Logan picked up a yoga class schedule and noticed
that there were some mistakes on it.
Circle all of the errors you can find.

Monday	Tuesday	Wednesday
Yogurt for Beginners 9:00–9:30 A.M. **Powder Yoga** 2:00–2:01 P.M.	**Weekend Yoga** 10:30–11:00 A.M. **Gentle Breese Yoga** 11:15–11:45 P.M.	**Sanshine Yoga** 6:30–7:00 A.M. **Yes to Yooga** 3:00–3:30 P.M.
Thursday	**Friday**	**Saturday**
Yoga, Yoga, Yoge! 8:45–9:15 A.M. **Yoga Hour** 6:00–6:15 P.M.	**Yoga for Yoo** 10:30–11:00 A.M. **Frienship Yoga** 10:30–11:00 A.M.	**Moonlight Yoga** 8:15–8:45 A.M. **Spirit Yoga** 2:00–2:30 P.S.

Answers

Mixed-up Message

Page 12

Dear Logan,
I will get meat and bread for
sandwiches. Bring your blue
kite and I'll bring my red one. I'll
meet you here at two. See you
soon!
Your friend,
Emmy

DearD iary

Page 13

Dear Diary,
Today was a great day. I went to the park lesS tudios
to meet some friends and make crafts. Someone
invited a new girl named Kayla to join us. She
just started here and is kind of shy. We started
talking and before you know it she was laughing and
joking around with me. I invited her to go swimming
with him tomorrow. She seems really nice and I'm
glad to have a new friend.
Talk to you later!
Neely

Neely's Nutty Note

Pages 14–15

Dear Grandma,
Thank you very much for the cool sweater! I love that
you made it yourself, and you used all my favorite colors.
I hope you can teach me to knit someday. Until then,
when I wear the sweater I'll think of you. Thanks again!
Love, Neely

Really Silly Rules

Page 17

1. run; 2. lock; 3. shower; 4. put; 5. wear; 6. clean; 7. tell

Boo, Team!

Page 18

Cheer 1	Cheer 2	Cheer 3
Feeling proud?	Stand up,	Wake up, everybody!
Yell it loud—	Let me hear you shout!	We're here to say
Go, team!	That's what teamwork	Our team's gonna win
	Is all about!	And today is the day!

Numbers & Letters

Page 19

Logan,
Good news—our team won! I waited for you after the game, but I didn't see you.
We are going for pizza now, so why don't you join us? (Unless you already ate!)
Hope to see you soon.
Riley

Sports Seen
Pages 20–21

A fan is wearing a "hoop girl" tee, and it should read "hoop girl"; "Ice Scream" should be Ice Cream; the ref is using cymbals; a player's tee has "anonymous" instead of her name; the game is played on a field, not a court; a player is wearing boots; two players are wearing the same numbers; Innerstar is misspelled; a player is holding up a "#2" finger; the scoreboard is wrong (it has incorrect numbers and wording).

Tack Track
Page 23

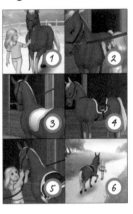

Horse Sense
Pages 24–25

Amber needs to exercise Angel at 9 a.m., Fleet at 11 a.m., Silver Sky at 1 p.m., Comet at 3 p.m., and Rio at 5 p.m.

Tricky Trophies
Pages 26–27

Innerstar University Riding Club Horse Show; 1st Place; cow trophy in horse case; 2nd Place; surfing trophy in horse case; Best in Show; 3rd Place; Grand Champion; horse trophy has 5 legs; 4th Place; 5th Place; 6th Place.

Apostrophe Catastrophe
Page 28

It's time for the Horse Lovers' Fun Show!
Mark your calendar because you won't want to miss out. It'll be July 2 at 3:00.
We'll have events, games, prizes, and even a parade.
Don't have a horse? Don't worry—we'll lend you one from the riding club's herd.
You can't beat that, so there's no excuse for not signing up.
You're going to have a blast, and your horse will be up to its ears in fun.
For more info, talk to Amber—she'll help you out.

Art-Show Showdown
Pages 30–31

A. 5; B. 4; C. 8; D. 3; E. 1; F. 7; G. 2; H. 6

Rave Review
Page 32

Here's our example, but you can rewrite the review in many different ways!
I thought this show was dazzling. The artist used a rainbow of colors in her artwork. One painting had splashes of crimson, aquamarine, and moss. Another painting was gigantic. One painting called *Floral Fantasy* had dozens of daisies all over it. I was thrilled seeing these paintings because they made me feel wonderful.

Craft Crunch

Page 33

1. Start with an empty toilet paper tube. **2.** Roll the tube in paw-print tissue paper, and secure along the tube with tape. **3.** Fill the wrapped tube with animal magnets, stickers, and a key chain. **4.** To be certain the contents stay in the tube, tie the tissue ends with ribbon.

Supplies Surprise

Pages 34–35

1. rubber stamps; 2. glitter; 3. paper;
4. inkpads; 5. glue; 6. paint; 7. felt;
8. watercolors; 9. crayons; 10. markers;
11. brushes; 12. rulers; 13. stickers; 14. clay

Ticket Trouble

Page 37

Admit One	U Shine Hall
"Dance Spectacular"	Row A
*Tuesday, April 1st	Seat 9
3:30 P.M.	$10.00

*Extra Credit: The poster shows Saturday at 3:00, but the ticket says Tuesday at 3:30.

Program Problems

Pages 38–39

Innerstar University's Dance Spectacular

Welcome Dance: All Dancers
An exciting number to thank you for coming to the show and to wish you a safe trip home (This is the first dance, so it should include words of welcome, and not wish guests a safe trip home first thing.)

Tapping Trio: Isabel, Cleo, Haley, and Annika
These three will amaze you with their jazzy routine set to a slow classic played on piano. (It says "trio" and "these three," but there are four dancers. Also, jazzy tap is not done to slow piano music.)

Jewelry-Box Ballerina: Neely
Start the music box and watch this ballerina pirouette in her tap shoes! (A ballerina can't pirouette in tap shoes. It should say toe shoes.)

Jazz Junction: Shelby and Chloe
A very contemporary dance that your great-great-grandma used to do. ("Contemporary" dance means from the present time and wouldn't be what your great-great-grandma did.)

Ballet Blossoms: Neely, Riley, Ella, and Linden
See these dancers turn into lovely blossoms from a vegetable tree. (There is no such thing as a vegetable tree!)

Farewell Finale: All Dancers
An opening act that showcases all of the dancers in today's show! (This is the last dance in the show, not the first.)

Inspiration Station

Pages 40–41

Dancing makes your spirit fly.
Happy birthday tutu you!
Dance makes the world go round.
Everyone has a little dancer in her heart.

A Chance to Dance
Page 42

Attention, dancers! Our next dance show will be called "Dancing Dreams." It will feature ballet, jazz, tap, and modern dance. Tryouts will be Friday at three o'clock in the auditorium. Please be sure to bring your music. To sign up, talk to Neely.

Name Game
Pages 44–45
1. Coconut; 2. Sugar; 3. Pepper;
4. Toasty; 5. Ginger; 6. Praline;
7. Chocolate Chip; 8. Honey

Not-Right Invite
Page 47

It's a Doggone Surprise Birthday Party for Amber!
Date: Wednesday, April 31
(There is no April 31!)
Time: 3 o'clock
(Or use just 3:00, but
you don't need both.)
Where: Pet Palooza
RSVP to Paige by Saturday
Don't tell Amber!
*Instead of a present, please
bring a dog or cat toy
to donate.*

Title Trouble
Page 51
2; 9; 1; 3; 4; 8; 5; 10; 6; 7

Maga-zany Mix
Pages 52–53

Tween Girls
August issue
• 51 Wonderful Christmas Ideas!
(The August issue wouldn't
show Christmas ideas.)
• Sweet Treats to Eat
• Learn to Be a Better Driver
(Tween girls aren't allowed
to drive!)

Messy Message
Page 46
Mrs. Chauncy called at one o'clock. She
wants to know whether Pet Palooza can
take care of her dog, Sweetie, while she
goes on vacation. She is leaving in a week.
I told her I did not know if there would be
room, but I would check. Would someone
please call her back? Her number is 555-
1876. She wants to know by tomorrow.
Thanks so much!

Instruction Obstruction
Pages 48–49

You can solve these more than one
way, but here are Logan's solutions.
Canines/Dogs
1. Walk dogs twice a day.
2. Always keep water dishes filled.
3. Brush dogs every other day.
4. Give each dog a toy.

Felines/Cats
1. Give cats treats every day.
2. Do not let cats outside.
3. Play with the cats.
4. Wash beds once a week.

Innerstar U Magazine
• Cool Girls on Campus
(There are no boys at ISU!)
• Sneak Peek at Dorm
Decor
• 55 Study Tips (This is
printed upside down.)

Pups & Kitties Magazine
• Crafts Your Pet Will Love
to Do (Pets can't do crafts!)
• Teach an Old Dog New
Tricks
• Furry Friends

All Sorts of Sports
Magazine
• Build a Birdhouse
(A birdhouse is not a
sports topic.)
• Badminton Is Good
• Running Shoes You
Can Use

Eagle Eye

Pages 54–55

The error is that Library is spelled wrong on the Innerstar University Library Computer Station sign. The other thing wrong is that the book titles aren't organized by subject or alphabetically by title.

Spill Check

Page 56
Gracie in the Big City

This book tells the story of Gracie, a girl who moves from her family's farm to live with her aunt in the big city for the summer. At first, Gracie has trouble making friends. She also misses the farm and the animals. She doesn't like how crowded and noisy the city is. Then she meets a girl named Janna in her apartment building. Janna shows Gracie all the things she loves about her city, like the parks and the museums. Gracie is sad when it's time to go back home, but she's happy when Janna says she'll come visit.

Muddled Menu

Pages 58–59

Cotton Candy; Cocoa Cloud; Minty Dream; Vanilla Surprise; Red Velvet; Blueberry Cobbler; Lemon Drop; Mint Chocolate; Strawberry Cream; Carrot Top; Grape Goodness; Sweet Honey; Triple Berry; Pumpkin Pie; Nut Crunch

Loony Shopping List

Page 60

These are the items you would use to make cupcakes: flour; sugar; vanilla; butter; milk; eggs; cocoa; chocolate chips; strawberries; blueberries; raspberries; bananas; lemon juice; peanut butter; honey; cream cheese

Wrong Receipt

Page 62

Welcome to Sweet Treats
It's the sweetest place at
Innerstar University

February 14

Strawberry cupcake	$3.00

(You don't need the word "dollars.")

Extra sprinkles	$0.50
Pink lemonade	$1.50
Iced tea	$1.50
Total	$6.50
Amount tendered	$7.00
Change due	$0.50

(You would get back only 50 cents.)

Thank you for coming. Have a nice day!

Recipe Mess-up

Page 61

1. recipe; 2. ingredients; 3. hands; 4. bowl; 5. spoon; 6. cupcake liners; 7. batter; 8. timer; 9. frosting

Screwy Signs

Pages 64–65

Dream Décor; Real Spirit Center; Stop; Please Keep Off the Grass; Please Don't Litter; Five-Points Plaza; Pedestrian Xing; Bravo Boutique; Girl Gear; Pajama Jam; Back to School!; Big Sale!; Sale!; Casual Closet; Real Beauty Salon; Today's Special; 10% Off; Good Sports Center; Glittering Gown; Shopping Square; Pet Palooza

Tees Teasers

Pages 66–67

(Page 66) nature nut; I (heart) puppies; soccer girl; girl power; horse crazy; flower power

(Page 67) it's a great day!; a dog is a girl's best friend; you're my best friend; too cute for my own good; better safe than sorry; kittens rule; reduce reuse recycle; later, gator!; one smart cookie; happy birthday; proud to be a bookworm; I love cheerleading

Hairstyle How-To

Page 68

4; 2; 1; 5; 3

Body Basics

Page 70

farms = arms; rose = toes; egg = leg; boulders = shoulders; pack = back; fleas = knees; dips = hips; drain = brain

Class Conundrum

Page 71

Monday	Tuesday	Wednesday
Yoga for Beginners 9:00-9:30 A.M. **Power Yoga** 2:00-2:30 P.M.	**Weekday Yoga** 10:30-11:00 A.M. **Gentle Breeze Yoga** 11:15-11:45 A.M.	**Sunshine Yoga** 6:30-7:00 A.M. **Yes to Yoga** 3:00-3:30 P.M.
Thursday	**Friday**	**Saturday**
Yoga, Yoga, Yoga! 8:45-9:15 A.M. **Yoga Hour** 6:00-7:00 P.M.	**Yoga for You** 10:30-11:00 A.M. **Friendship Yoga** 10:30-11:00 A.M. (Same time as Yoga for You.)	**Moonlight Yoga** 8:15-8:45 P.M. **Spirit Yoga** 2:00-2:30 P.M.

INNERSTARU.COM

The puzzle fun continues online!

Use the code below for access to
even more puzzles and activities.

Go online to innerstarU.com/puzzle
and enter this code: MISTEAKS

Basic System Requirements:
Windows: Internet Explorer 7 or 8, Firefox 2.0+, Google Chrome
Mac: Safari 4.0+
Monitor Resolution: Optimized for 1024 x 768 or larger
Flash Version 10 and high-speed Internet required

Requirements may change. Visit www.innerstarU.com for
full requirements and latest updates.

Important Information:
Recommended for girls 8 and up. American Girl reserves the right
to modify, restrict access to, or discontinue www.innerstarU.com
at any time, in its sole discretion, without prior notice.

Here are some other American Girl books you might like:

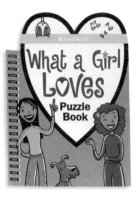

❑ I read it.

❑ I read it.

❑ I read it.

❑ I read it.

❑ I read it.

❑ I read it.